CW01086405

This book is dedicated to:

Ethan

To share on your special day,

and for everyday after!

The Knock, Knock! Jokes

AND

Pirates

COLORING

Book

For Kids!

This Copy of

The
Knock Knock Jokes
and
Pirates Coloring Book for Kids!

BELONGS TO:

Welcome to Avery Sinclair's wonderful

Knock Knock Jokes and

Pirates Coloring Book for Kids!

This book has over 200 Laugh-out-Loud Knock Knock Jokes, and 20 pirates & backgrounds from all over the world just waiting for you to color them in! You can even color in the words and Letters in this book! And... if you really want to show off, do you think you can color in the pirates, ships, and animals while someone reads the belly bursting Knock Knock Jokes to you?

Avery Sinclair doesn't think so, but Let's see if we can prove him wrong, arrrgh matey?!!

can you spot the 5 differences in these 2 pictures?

Knock Knock. Who's There? Kanye. Kanye who?
Kanye invite me in already it's freezing out here!

Knock Knock. Who's There? Yukon. Yukon who?
Yukon go away and come back another time.

Knock Knock. Who's There? Zippy. Zippy who?
Zippy de-doo-dah to you too!

Knock Knock. Who's There? Ida. Ida who?
It's not Ida who, it's Idaho!

Knock Knock. Who's There? Hatch. Hatch who? Bless you.

Knock Knock. Who's There? Stan. Stan who?
Stan back, I'm going to sneeze.

Knock Knock. Who's There? Agatha. Agatha who?
Agatha terrible toothache!

Knock Knock. Who's There? Atomic. Atomic who?
Atomic ache.

Knock Knock. Who's There? Aileen. Aileen who?
Aileen Dover and fell down.

Knock Knock. Who's There? Sarah. Sarah who?
Sarah doctor in the house?

Arrrgh matey!
How about a
touch of color?

Knock Knock. Who's There? Ewan. Ewan who?
No one else, just me.

Knock Knock. Who's There? Arfur. Arfur who?
Arfur got...

Knock Knock. Who's There? Amy. Amy who?
Amy fraid I've forgotten.

Knock Knock. Who's There? Zoom. Zoom who?
Zoom do you expect?

Knock Knock. Who's There? Ama. Ama who?
Ama not going to tell you!

Knock Knock. Who's There? Anna. Anna who?
Anna one, two, three, four...

Knock Knock. Who's There? Howard. Howard who?
Howard you like to let me let me in?

Knock Knock. Who's There? Auto. Auto who?
You auto know me by now!

Knock Knock. Who's There? Emma. Emma who?
Emma destined to stay out here forever?

Knock Knock. Who's There? Any. Any who?
Hey don't change the subject.

NOW THIS SHIP COULD DO WITH A LICK OF COLOR!

Knock Knock. Who's There? Stewart. Stewart who?
Stewart supposed to let me in when I knocked.

Knock Knock. Who's There? Eyes. Eyes who?
Eyes got loads more knock knock jokes for you!

Knock Knock. Who's There? Tank. Tank who?
You're welcome.

Knock Knock. Who's There? Linda. Linda who?
Linda hand and open this door will ya?

Knock Knock. Who's There? Says. Says who?
Says me, that's who!

Knock Knock. Who's There? Omar. Omar who?
Omar goodness gracious - wrong door!

Knock Knock. Who's There? Izzy. Izzy who?
Izzy come, izzy go.

Knock Knock. Who's There? Lettuce. Lettuce who?
Lettuce tell you some knock knock jokes.

Knock Knock. Who's There? Doris. Doris who?
Doris open so I'm coming in!

Knock Knock. Who's There? Diana. Diana who?
Diana third, can I have a drink please?

Oink, oink matey!
How about you
color my snout?

Knock Knock. Who's There? Stella. Stella who?
Stella no idea who I am do you?

Knock Knock. Who's There? Harry. Harry who?
Harry up and answer this door!

Knock Knock. Who's There? Sia. Sia who?
Sia later, alligator.

Knock Knock. Who's There? Paul. Paul who?
Paul hard, the door's stuck again.

Knock Knock. Who's There? Patsy. Patsy who?
Patsy dog on the head, he likes it.

Knock Knock. Who's There? Oscar. Oscar who?
Oscar a stupid question, you get a stupid answer.

Knock Knock. Who's There? Olive. Olive who? Olive you too!

Knock Knock. Who's There? Me too. Me too who?
Me to you, you to me.

Knock Knock. Who's There? You. You who?
Yooooo-whooooo!

Knock Knock. Who's There? Mandy. Mandy who?
Mandy the lifeboats, we're sinking.

what color do
you think this ship
should be?

Knock, Knock. Who's there? Candice. Candice who?
Candice joke get any worse?

Knock, knock. Who's there? Lena. Lena who?
Lena a little closer, and I'll tell you another!

Knock, Knock. Who's there? Show. Show who?
I'll show you once you open the door.

Knock, knock. Who's there? Adore. Adore who?
Adore is between us, please open it!

Knock, Knock. Who's there? Leon. Leon who?
Leon me, when you're not strong!

Knock, knock. Who's there? Go. Go who?
Alright, alright I'm going already!

Knock, Knock. Who's there? Wah. Wah who?
What are you so excited about?!

Knock knock. Who's there? Annie. Annie who?
Is Annie body home?

Knock Knock. Who's there? Norma Lee. Norma Lee who?
Normally I ring the doorbell.

Knock knock. Who's there? Cee. Cee who?
You Cee me standing here and still won't open the door?

captain parrot the pirate needs some color!

can you spot the 5 differences in these 2 pictures?

Knock, Knock. Who's there? Spell. Spell who? W-H-O.

Knock, knock. Who's there? Lisa. Lisa who?
Lisa the talking, more of the door opening please!

Knock, Knock. Who's there? Major. Major who?
Major day with this joke haven't I?

Knock, Knock. Who's there? Leash. Leash who?
Leash you could do is open the door!

Knock, Knock. Who's there? Cash. Cash who?
No thanks, but I'll take a peanut if you have one!

Knock, knock. Who's there? Carry. Carry who?
Carry my bags up the stairs please!

Knock, Knock. Who's there? Bina. Bina who?
Bina a while I've been standing here now...

Knock, knock. Who's there? Glenda. Glenda who?
Glenda hand and open this door will ya?

Knock, Knock. Who's there? Broccoli? Broccoli who?
Broccoli doesn't have a last name, silly.

Knock, knock. Who's there? Goliath. Goliath who?
Goliath down, you look-eth tired!

A shark in the sea? what color should it be?

Knock Knock. Who's There? Ivor. Ivor who?
Ivor sore hand from knocking on your door!

Knock Knock. Who's There? Lettuce. Lettuce who?
Lettuce in, won't you?

Knock Knock. Who's There? Donald. Donald who?
Donald back on opening that door now.

Knock Knock. Who's There? Doctor. Doctor who?
No, he's not a real doctor at all!

Knock Knock. Who's There? Sultan. Sultan who?
Sultan Pepper.

Knock Knock. Who's There? Thermos. Thermos who?
Thermos be a better knock knock joke than this.

Knock Knock. Who's There? Ocelot. Ocelot who?
You Ocelot of questions, don't you?

Knock Knock. Who's There? Dismay. Dismay who?
Dismay be a joke, but it didn't make me laugh.

Knock Knock. Who's There? Dwayne. Dwayne who?
Dwayne no way I'm getting in here is there?

Knock Knock. Who's There? Broken pencil.
Broken pencil who? Nevermind, it's pointless.

monkey the matey found some hidden treasure!

Knock Knock. Who's There? Hal. Hal who?
Well Hallo to you too!

Knock Knock. Who's There? Beets. Beets who?
Beets me, I forgot the joke.

Knock Knock. Who's There? Train. Train who?
Someone should train you how to open the door!

Knock Knock. Who's There? Ether. Ether who?
Ether bunny.

Knock Knock. Who's There? Nanya. Nanya who?
Nanya your business!

Knock Knock. Who's There? Quacker. Quacker who?
Quacker 'nother bad joke and I'm off!

Knock Knock. Who's There? Rhoda. Rhoda who?
Rhoda boat as fast as you can!

Knock Knock. Who's There? Rufus. Rufus who?
The Rufus the most important part of your house!

Knock Knock. Who's There? X. X who?
X-tremely pleased to meet you!

Knock Knock. Who's There? Banana. Banana who?
Banana split so ice creamed.

sailing across the
wavy blue sea!
what is missing?

Knock Knock. Who's There? Howard. Howard who? Howard I Know?

Knock Knock. Who's There? Noah. Noah who? Noah don't know either.

Knock Knock. Who's There? Kent. Kent who? Kent you tell?

Knock Knock. Who's There? Owl say. Owl say who? Actually, Owl say HOOT!

Knock Knock. Who's There? Wooden shoe. Wooden shoe who? Wooden shoe like to Know?

Knock Knock. Who's There? Yora. Yora who? Ah thanks, you're lots of fun too!

Knock Knock. Who's There? Freddie. Freddie who? Freddie or not, here I come.

Knock Knock. Who's There? Dozen. Dozen who? Dozen anybody want to let me in?

Knock Knock. Who's There? Toodle. Toodle who? Oh, okay bye then.

Knock Knock. Who's There? Who. Who who? Bad echo in here, isn't there?

shiver me whiskers!
This little kitty is a
pity with no color!

Knock, Knock. Who's there? Youann. Youann who?
Nope, it's just me today!

Knock, knock. Who's there? Egg. Egg who?
Eggstremely disappointed you don't recognize me.

Knock, Knock. Who's there? Zinc. Zinc who?
It's zinc or swim!

Knock, knock. Who's there? A herd. A herd who?
A herd you were home so I came over!

Knock, Knock Who's there? Alex. Alex who?
Alex-plain when you open the door!

Knock, knock. Who's there? Otter. Otter who?
You Otter know by now!

Knock, Knock. Who's there? Harlow. Harlow who?
Harlow can you go?

Knock, knock. Who's there? No. No who?
I know you, that's why I'm here!

Knock, Knock. Who's there? Arthur. Arthur who?
Arthur all that time you open the door!

Knock, knock. Who's there? Andy. Andy who?
Andy takes forever to answer a door!

This is too big of a ship to be so dull, don't ya think?

can you spot the 5 differences in these 2 pictures?

Knock, Knock. Who's there? Orange. Orange who?
Orange you going to let me in?

Knock, knock. Who's there? Chicken. Chicken who?
Chicken your pockets for your keys!

Knock, Knock. Who's there! This suits. This suits who?
Thanks, I bought it yesterday!

Knock, Knock. Who's there! Savannah! Savannah who?
Savannah ever going to open this door?

Knock, Knock. Who's there? Toucan. Toucan who?
Toucan play that game, who's there?

Knock, Knock. Who's there? Sacha ! Sacha who?
Sacha fuss to get here!

Knock, Knock. Who's there? Ears. Ears Who?
Ears another knock, knock joke for you.

Knock, Knock Who's there? Watson. Watson Who?
Watson new with you?

Knock Knock. Who's There? Andrew. Andrew who?
I didn't draw anyone.

Knock Knock. Who's There? Boo. Boo who?
No need to cry, it's just a joke!

This bear thinks
some treasure
is near!

Knock Knock. Who's There? Colleen. Colleen who?
Colleen your room, it's filthy.

Knock Knock. Who's There? Defence. Defence who.
Defence has a hole in it, you should check it out.

Knock Knock. Who's There? Alma. Alma who?
Alma candy's gone!

Knock Knock. Who's There? Amos. Amos who?
Amos-quito bit me.

Knock Knock. Who's There? N. E. N.E. who?
N.E. body you like, let me in!

Knock Knock. Who's There? Max. Max who?
Max no difference, open the door!

Knock Knock. Who's There? Deduct. Deduct who?
Donald Deduct.

Knock Knock. Who's There? What. What who?
Where? When? Why? How?

Knock Knock. Who's There? Amanda. Amanda who?
Amanda you take a long time to answer your door!

Knock Knock. Who's There? Cozy. Cozy who?
Cozy who's Knocking, will you?

12

Decisions, decisions.
so many colors to
choose from...!

Knock Knock. Who's there? Thanks. Thanks who?
Thank you too!

Knock knock. Who's there? Etch. Etch who?
I'm coming at you too!

Knock Knock. Who's there? How. How who?
I'm good thanks, how are you?

Knock, knock Who's there? Chin. Chin who?
Chin up, this is the last knock, knock joke.

Knock, knock Who's there? Orange. Orange who?
Orange you glad I didn't say banana?

Knock, knock Who's there? Eden. Eden who?
Eden my dinner at the moment, I'll come back!

Knock, Knock. Who's there? Barbara. Barbara who?
Barbara black sheep have you any wool?

Knock, knock. Who's there? Figs. Figs who?
Figs the doorbell, it's broken!

Knock, Knock. Who's there? Nobel. Nobel who?
No bell, that's why I knocked!

Knock, knock. Who's there? Luke. Luke who?
Luke through the peephole and you'll find out!

I'm safely on shore,
now I sure could do
with some color!

Knock Knock. Who's There? Consumption. Consumption who? Consumption be done about all these Knock Knock jokes?

Knock Knock. Who's There? Tuna Fish. Tuna Fish who? You can tune a piano, but you can't tuna fish.

Knock Knock. Who's There? Cows. Cows who? No Cows moo.

Knock Knock. Who's There? Conner. Conner who? Conner open the door or what?

Knock Knock. Who's There? Jupiter. Jupiter who? Jupiter hurry and answer the door!

Knock Knock. Who's There? Ivan. Ivan who? Ivan had to wait outside so long before.

Knock Knock. Who's There? Kanga. Kanga who? Nope, it's pronounced Kangaroo!

Knock Knock. Who's There? Wooden. Wooden who? Wooden you like to know?

Knock Knock. Who's There? Harriet. Harriet who? Harriet all my lunch, I'm starving.

Knock Knock. Who's There? Closure. Closure who? Closure door on the way out!

HOW many Faces can you spot in this picture?

Knock Knock. Who's There? Simon. Simon who?
Simon on this side of the door, why?

Knock Knock. Who's There? Isadore. Isadore who?
Isadore open or locked?

Knock Knock. Who's There? Sis. Sis who?
Sis anyway to treat a friend?

Knock Knock. Who's There? Don. Don who?
Don mess around, and just open the door!

Knock Knock. Who's There? Ferdie. Ferdie who?
Ferdie last time, open this door!

Knock Knock. Who's There? Abbot. Abbot who?
Abbot time you let me in!

Knock Knock. Who's There? Earl. Earl who?
Earl be glad to tell you if you open this door.

Knock Knock. Who's There? Juan. Juan who?
Juan of these days you'll find out.

Knock Knock. Who's There? Jude. Jude who?
It's pronounced Judo.

Knock Knock. Who's There? Isabel. Isabel who?
Isabel broken? Because I had to knock.

He he heee...
This one might take
koala color in!

can you spot the 5 differences in these 2 pictures?

Knock, Knock. Who's there? CIA. CIA w—
Excuse me, we're asking the questions here.

Knock, knock. Who's there? Disco. Disco who?
Disco's on for far too long.

Knock, Knock. Who's there? To. To who?
It's actually To 'Whom'.

Knock, knock. Who's there? Water. Water Who?
Water you waiting for? Answer the door!

Knock, Knock. Who's there? Want. Want who?
Want, who, three, four, five...

Knock, knock. Who's there? Interrupting Cow.
Interrupting c—Moooo!

Knock, Knock. Who's there? Owls say. Owls say who?
They do but I still need to come in.

Knock, knock. Who's there? Ho-ho. Ho-ho who?
Your Santa impression needs work.

Knock, Knock. Who's there? Alien. Alien who?
How many aliens do you know?

Knock, Knock. Who's there? Control Freak.
Co— You should say, "Control freak who" now.

He he heee...
This one might take
koala color in!

**Knock Knock. Who's There? Scold. Scold who?
Scold outside.**

Knock Knock. Who's There? Justice. Justice who?
Justice this once let's skip the knock knock jokes please!

**Knock Knock. Who's There? Anna. Anna who?
Anna Partridge in a pear treeeee...**

Knock Knock. Who's There? Obie. Obie who?
Oh behave and let me in already!

**Knock Knock. Who's There? Sarah. Sarah who?
Sarah 'nother way into this building?**

Knock Knock. Who's There? Ice cream. Ice cream who?
Ice cream if you don't let me in.

**Knock Knock. Who's There? You. You who?
You who! Is there anybody there?**

Knock Knock. Who's There? Sarah. Sarah who?
Sarah chance I could come inside?

Knock Knock. Who's There? Ken. Ken who? Ken I come in?

Knock Knock. Who's There? Theodore. Theodore who?
Theodore wasn't open so I knocked!

If there's hidden
treasure, you can bet
this rabbit will grab it!

Knock Knock. Who's There? Isaiah. Isaiah who?
Isaiah, would you mind letting me in?

Knock Knock. Who's There? Bacon. Bacon who?
Bacon a cake just for you!

Knock Knock. Who's There? Jess. Jess who?
Jess open the door already!

Knock Knock. Who's There? Weirdo. Weirdo who?
Weirdo these doors come from?

Knock Knock. Who's There? He. He who?
He who laughs a lot laughs last!

Knock Knock. Who's There? Justin. Justin who?
Justin time for dinner!

Knock Knock. Who's There? Disguise. Disguise who?
Disguise jokes are awful.

Knock Knock. Who's There? Minnie. Minnie who?
Minnie people ask me that.

Knock Knock. Who's There? Kung. Kung who?
It's pronounced Kung-Fu actually.

Knock Knock. Who's There? Biscuit. Biscuit who?
Biscuit out here quick it's an emergency!

can you spot the 5 differences in these 2 pictures?

Knock, Knock. Who's there? Justin. Justin who?
Justin the neighborhood, thought I'd drop by.

Knock, knock. Who's there? Justin. Justin who?
Justin case you didn't hear me the first time!

Knock, Knock. Who's there? Pee. Pee who?
Pee-yew it stinks in here!

Knock, knock. Who's there? Ben. Ben who?
Ben knocking all morning, let me in!

Knock, Knock. Who's there? Sacha. Sacha who?
Sacha lot of questions!

Knock, knock. Who's there? Dave. Dave who?
Dave done really well with your door knocker!

Knock, Knock. Who's there? Les. Les who?
Les go out!

Knock, knock. Who's there? Heave. Heave who?
Come on, the door's not that heavy!

Knock, Knock. Who's there? Churchill. Churchill who?
Churchill be the best place for the wedding.

Knock, knock. Who's there? Anita. Anita who?
Anita get inside!

19

Thanks For Reading!

Just a quick message to thank you so much for picking up one of our books! Our sincere hope is that this book has given you the value we always look to provide, and hope we can continue to produce quality books that will in any way contribute to a better quality of life for our readers.

We are a small independent publisher based in London, UK and we work with talented authors from around the world, who dedicate every ounce of their effort to craft these memorable books for your reading pleasure.

The author of this title would love to hear about your experience with the book, and your review will go a long way to provide them with the insight and encouragement they need to keep creating the kind of books you want to read.

Your Opinion Makes a Real Difference.

If you want to let us know what you thought about the book, please visit the Amazon website and give us your review.
We read every single review, no matter how long or short!

Thanks again and until the next time....

HAPPY READING!

Printed in Great Britain
by Amazon

66300054R00031